# Jimbo and the Jet-set



Written and Illustrated by Peter Maddocks

Macdonald Purnell

ISBN 0 361 07145 0

Licensed by BBC Enterprises Limited
Published 1986 by Purnell Books
a division of Macdonald and Co. (Publishers) Limited
Maxwell House, 74 Worship Street, London EC2A 2EN
a BPCC plc company
Made and printed in Great Britain by
Purnell and Sons (Book Production) Limited
Paulton, Bristol BS18 5LQ

Jimbo had been flying all night. He was tired, dusty and above all he was late for his arrival at London Airport.

"I bet I'm the last plane home," he grumbled as he blinked through the darkness.

He was about to say "Hello, London," when suddenly there was a blinding flash of lightning followed by a great rolling clap of thunder.

"That's all I need, now," said Jimbo, "a stormy landing."

"Gosh, that lightning flash has made my eyes go funny," said Jimbo, "what's that ahead of me? It looks like a very strange object — good grief! It looks like a flying saucer!"

"It **is** a flying saucer! — hello, London," Jimbo yelled. "Can you hear me? Hello, hello, come in, London!"

There was a pop, crackle and fizz on the radio followed by the sleepy voice of the Chief's assistant controller.

"Hello, Jimbo, we can hear you — give us your position please, Jimbo," yawned the voice.

"Give me the chief controller, quickly," cried Jimbo. "I've just seen a flying saucer."

The sleepy assistant giggled and leaning back over his chair he said:

"It's Jimbo for you, Chief — I warn you, he's up to his tricks again."

"Give me that microphone," said the Chief. "I want words with **that** plane . . ."

"Jimbo," said the Chief, angrily, "wherever have you been? It's way past our bedtime."

"Sorry, Chief," replied Jimbo anxiously. "I've been delayed by bad weather — and what's more I think I've seen a flying saucer."

"Of course you have, Jimbo," mocked the Chief. "Was it yellow with red spots?"

"No, Chief — as a matter of fact it was an orange colour!"

"Just you get down here at once," screamed the chief controller. "Orange flying saucers, indeed!"

"But, Chief," stammered Jimbo. "Oh never mind, permission to land please," he said sadly.

"Permission granted," replied the Chief. "And about time too." Then he turned to his assistant and said:

"Be a good chap and fetch me a nice cup of cocoa, while I get this naughty little plane down and settled for the night."

"Righto, Chief," said the assistant. "I won't be long." With that he vanished through the door of the control room into the night.

"He should have taken an umbrella," said the Chief to himself as he watched the lightning flashes through the window of the control tower.

"This storm is getting worse. My goodness! What's that?" Suddenly the whole control tower was shaking.

"What's going on?" he cried.

The shaking and shimmering got worse and worse until all the windows rattled and a strange yellow light filled the control room.

Then, with a terrific jolt the control tower began to climb skywards, slowly, like a huge lift in a shaft of yellow light. The chief controller clung on to his desk for dear life.

"What's going on?" muttered the Chief, nervously. "It must be an earthquake. I'm getting out of here." He rushed to the exit door only to find it locked and bolted — from the outside. The control tower continued to move slowly upwards . . .

Meanwhile, Jimbo was trying to find his approach position for landing but because of the raging storm and low clouds all he could do was fly around in circles . . .

"Hello, hello," he shouted. "Can you hear me down there?" But all Jimbo could hear was the pop, pop, crackle of a radio followed by violent flashes of lightning and rolling thunderclaps.

"I'll never land at this rate," thought Jimbo.

The Chief meanwhile, locked in his rising control tower, tried every switch on his desk to find someone to talk to — he was so terrified, even Jimbo would have been welcome.

"Come in, somebody!" he screamed. Suddenly the control tower jerked to a halt — CLUNK. Followed by silence.

Everything was quiet. The flashing lights stopped flashing. All the computer codes on the control tower vanished from the screens, and the Chief still didn't know what was happening.

"Help!" cried the chief controller, followed by a much louder scream: "HELP!"

The Chief, now frantic with fear, became very angry — and wiggling every switch on his desk he screamed:

"Jimbo, this is something to do with you, isn't it? This is one of your silly larks — I'll get you for this, just you wait!"

Suddenly the Chief stopped talking because he noticed a tapping sound coming from the window — outside. Knock, knock, knock . . .

A deep voice echoed around the control room: "Hello in there, can you hear me speaking? . . . I command you to answer — speak!"

The knocking on the window continued.

The poor Chief hid beneath his desk, trembling with fear.

"Speak," boomed the voice once more. "Is this the planet Mars? Answer me, quickly."

"No! Your wierdship — er, your highness — gulp no, no," stuttered the quivering Chief from beneath the desk. "This is Earth, not Mars — the planet Earth."

There was complete silence for a full minute followed again by the flat, low voice:

"Sorry to have bothered you, Earthman — we have got the wrong planet. I bid you a spaceman's farewell."

"And a spaceman's farewell to you — sir," stammered the Chief, now peeping over the top of the desk . . .

And there he saw the face of the space creature — all green and yellow, shimmering in a strange light.

"Farewell, Earthman," repeated the creature. It vanished into the night leaving the wide-eyed and open-mouthed Chief staring into space.

As the face disappeared from the window so the light changed back to yellow, and suddenly the Chief was aware of a downward movement. The control tower had started its descent to Earth again.

Outside, the skies had cleared and Jimbo could clearly see the landing strip laid out before him.

"And about time, too," he thought. "I was beginning to think I'd never get down."

Runway Four was now clear, and the only visible sign of the terrible storm was the glistening wet surface which threw up a fine spray of water as Jimbo safely touched down to land.

"Thank goodness for that," said Jimbo. "I'm home at last."

Jimbo was greeted by Tommy Tow-Truck who had wearily come out to tow him back to his hangar.

"Good to see you, Jimbo," said Tommy. "We've had the most terrible stormy night."

"Don't I know it!" said Jimbo. "I've been flying around up there waiting to get permission to land, but there was no answer from the control tower," growled Jimbo, angrily. "Where is everybody?"

"I'm not surprised," said Tommy Tow-Truck, towing Jimbo across the runway. "The control tower was struck by lightning ten minutes ago — the controller's assistant was in the canteen getting the Chief his bedtime cup of cocoa at the time. He's gone to see if the Chief is okay."

Inside the control tower the Chief had just experienced a final bump and the windows rattled once more as it struck the ground.

"I'm down," he shouted. "Back on my beloved airfield — let me out of here!"

The door of the control tower flew open, revealing the Chief's assistant, now wide awake, standing in the doorway with a hot cup of cocoa in his hand.

"Are you okay, Chief?" he said. "The lightning struck the tower and the whole place was bathed in yellow light — very creepy it was — I nearly dropped your cocoa."

"Thank goodness it's you," screamed the Chief as he barged past his assistant, knocking the cocoa flying. "Let me out of here!" Seeing Jimbo, the Chief raced towards the little plane.

"Jimbo, my friend," he screamed. "I've seen the green spaceman!"

"Jimbo — forgive me, you did see a flying saucer, and I've seen the spaceman — 'Speak to me, earthman,' he cried," said the chief controller. Jimbo and Tommy looked at each other, wondering if the Chief was ill.

"That lightning has made him a bit light headed, Tommy," said Jimbo.

"I should go straight to bed if I were you, Chief," said Tommy, slowly moving away.

"Yes, but first a final farewell to my friends in space," said the Chief walking out towards the end of the runway, his arms outstretched.

"Farewell, spaceman — maybe we shall meet again in another galaxy!"

"Hurry up and put my hangar light out," said Jimbo, "before he starts seeing spacemen in here. Goodnight, Tommy," said Jimbo.

"Goodnight, Jimbo," said Tommy.

"Goodnight, spaceman," shouted the Chief.